What if animals could tell us their tales?

They can in ... **The PERSIAN PLOT**

A Tale about Courage

Written and illustrated by
T. F. Marsh

Faith KiDs

Equipping Kids for Life!

H ave you ever wondered, *really* wondered, what you would do if you had to make the most important choice ever? Well, a beauty queen taught me the difference between a good choice and a bad choice. Oh, yeah, my name's Chamelia, your Tale Teller. A color-changing chameleon, I might add. Here's my groovy tale, just for you!

On my sixteenth birthday, my dad and I were walking through the palace garden. He had made an important decision.

"Chamelia," he said, "you're free to walk through this entire garden alone. But be careful what you say and do, or it may come back to harm you."

"Oh, I will, I will!" I shouted as I gave him a big hug. "Wow, this is the *best* present ever. Freedom!"

The next morning, I woke up especially early and slipped on my flip-flops. I couldn't wait to walk through the garden *alone*. Far out!

As I daydreamed about how my friends would envy me, suddenly something pulled me through a hole in the stone wall!

"We've got to hurry!" whispered a garbled voice just ahead of me in the darkness.

"Hey, who *are* you?" I asked the stranger who was pulling me through a dark maze. "And where are you taking me?"

There was just more of that muddled talk. Something about being late. Finally, the stranger pulled me into a brightly lit room. And there I met my kidnapper. Yuck . . . one of those gross palace roaches I'd heard tales about.

P lease, my dear, the beauty contest will be starting soon," he stuttered. "I am Sir Crumsby, and you're a beautiful girl. Now, quickly, I've brought your gown. I'm counting on *you* to win!"

I was flattered. I blushed a radical shade of pink. "Wait a minute!" I said. "Who's putting on this beauty contest?"

"Why, King Xerxes, of course!" he warbled.

As we zoomed through more roach tunnels, Crumsby explained.

"King Xerxes made a costly decision a while back. He called for Vashti, his beautiful queen, to come show herself to his palace guests. But she refused. So, angry and embarrassed, he sent her away. Now he's lonely and wants another queen. *That* is why he's holding a beauty contest!"

C rumsby led me to a large room filled with beautiful young ladies. Why, this place was really hip.

Crumsby cleared his throat. "The king will choose one lady to be his new queen. And I need *you* to win. You see, queens give special privileges to whomever they please— even to us hungry roaches."

"That's crazy!" I shouted. "I'm a chameleon, not a queen! I'm out of this contest."

But Crumsby wasn't listening. He was staring at one of the contestants. He squirmed. "Oh, no. It's Esther, the new arrival. I've heard plenty about her. She's the most beautiful woman here. And she's already gained special privileges from Hegai, keeper of the women. But don't fear, my dear. A Persian king would *never* choose a Jewish woman for his queen."

W hy wouldn't he choose a Jewish woman?" I asked.

Crumsby shuddered. "Because the Jews and Persians follow different laws, a Jewish queen would be trouble. But don't worry. With *you* entered, we can't lose."

Well, I wasn't entering any beauty contest, but I *would* dress up and stick around to see what would happen.

Each lady prepared herself for twelve months. Then, one by one, each contestant was taken to the king . . . then brought back. Finally, it was Esther's turn to go to the king's palace.

The hours passed slowly as we waited. What was happening? Suddenly, the news was sounded. The king had chosen his new queen. Hey, it was Esther—she'd won! And the king didn't even know she was Jewish. Groovy!

E very morning I went to the palace to watch Esther. Every evening I returned home and told my parents the latest news.

Then, one morning Esther was troubled. Her cousin Mordecai, the gatekeeper, had overheard two men planning to kill the king!

Esther went to the king and told him everything Mordecai had overheard. Immediately, the two men were punished. That day, everything was written in a book of records to be remembered. Mordecai had saved the king.

Whew! All troubles seemed to be over for that day—until I bumped into the palace snake. He was really creepy. I turned white with fright!

"My master Haman doesn't like that Mordecai," he hissed. "Mordecai's a troublemaker!"

Who's Master Haman?" I asked timidly.

He grinned slyly. "Why, he helps the king rule over the land, of course. Everyone bows down to him. Everyone except that Jewish gatekeeper, Mordecai. He won't bow down . . . and that makes my master mad! But don't worry, my dear. Master Haman knows what to say and do."

Well, I managed to wiggle away from that creepy snake's coils. But no sooner was he out of sight than I bumped into the other palace pet—the crazy mongoose.

"Looky! Looky!" he chattered. "Master Haman is with the king. And is *he* angry with that Mordecai! I'll bet he's gonna get him, and get him good."

"Oh, yeah, what's he gonna do?" I asked, turning red with rage.

W atch! Watch!" he chattered. "Master Haman knows what to say and do!"

He was right. Haman had hatched a wicked Persian plot to destroy Mordecai and the Jewish people! Haman said that the Jewish people were different from all others in the kingdom. They followed their own laws, and they didn't keep the king's laws. He even said that they didn't have any worth to the king, except for their money. They must all be destroyed!

Then the king gave Haman his ring as permission to do whatever he chose with the Jewish people and their money. So Haman gave the order: On the thirteenth day of the twelfth month, all of the Jews would die! Ugh, that Haman. I didn't like him at all.

T he terrible news spread throughout the land. The Jews were in mourning. Then I had a terrible thought. Esther was a Jew! Would she be destroyed too? I had to find her.

When I reached her chambers, I found her bowed down and troubled. Suddenly, I heard a familiar voice. Hey, it was Crumsby!

"Have you heard the news?" I asked, filled with the blues.

"Yes," he answered, twitching. "But maybe Esther became queen for such a time as this. Mordecai just sent her some wise counsel. She is to ask the king to save her people's lives. Besides, her life is in trouble too. No matter what the consequence, she must ask the king for their deliverance."

What would Esther say and do?

Q uickly, she sent Mordecai her reply. She would see the king. But first, all of the Jews were to fast on her behalf for three days. She and her palace maids would do the same. Then she would go to the king. Interrupting the king could mean death. But if she perished, she perished.

Crumsby gulped. "This choice could come back to harm her."

But I had a little more faith. "Don't worry, Crumsby. I think she knows what to say and do."

Well, after the three days of fasting, Esther went to see the king. And what was her consequence for interrupting him? Why, she found favor with him. The king asked her to state her request. She asked him to attend a special banquet—and Haman was invited. Wait! Haman was invited too?

I can't believe it!" I blurted. "Why is *he* invited?"

Crumsby twisted his antennae and grinned. "I guess we'll just have to go find out for ourselves. And while we're there, lots of food for us!"

Haman joined the king at Esther's banquet. After the king had eaten, he asked Esther to state her request. Whatever she wanted, he would give to her.

Esther silently turned away to think. She seemed very concerned. Finally, she turned back and invited the king *and* Haman to return the next day to a second banquet. Then she would give her request to the king.

"I guess we'll meet back here tomorrow," Crumsby crunched away. "The only thing better than one banquet is two!"

I n the middle of the night, I heard rustling outside my window. I panicked until I heard crunching. Yep, it was Crumsby.

"What are you doing here?" I whispered. "Do you know what time it is?"

"No time to explain," he trembled. "Mordecai is in big trouble. I followed Haman home earlier tonight. I couldn't help it. He was dropping crumbs everywhere. Anyway, Haman has built a giant gallows—to hang Mordecai!"

As fast as we could, we scurried to the king's chamber. Only *he* could stop Haman's ghoulish plot.

We found the king restless. The book of records was being read to him. He was being told that Mordecai had never been rewarded for saving his life.

Suddenly the door opened.

"Oh, no!" I shouted. "It's Haman!"

*S*miling, the king asked Haman what he should do to reward someone who pleased him.

Haman grinned with self-pride, thinking the king was talking about him! He replied that the person should receive majestic clothes, a crown, and a ride on the king's horse.

The king agreed. *Mordecai* deserved all of those things. And Haman was chosen to serve him! Haman gulped.

All that day, Mordecai was exalted throughout the city. And Haman? Well, *his* troubles had just begun.

You see, we soon found ourselves at Esther's second banquet. The snake and mongoose had followed Haman in too. After we had eaten, the king once again asked Esther to tell him her request. Esther had to make her most important choice ever. Her people's lives had to come before her own. She asked for her people's lives, and hers, to be spared from Haman's plot to destroy all Jews. For *she* was Jewish also!

Immediately, the king became angry. How dare Haman plot to destroy his Esther!

I'll bet the king knows what to say and do," smiled Crumsby as he crunched and munched. He was right. The king made his decision. Today, not Mordecai, but *Haman* would be hanged on the gallows! The guards led Haman away. His bad choice brought him harm. Next, the palace taxidermist came and took the snake and mongoose away. Ugh!

Mordecai was then given Haman's old position. With his new authority, he could make rules allowing the Jews to defend themselves. Esther's most important choice had saved her people. Her good choice brought her blessing.

I sighed in relief. "Now Esther and the king will live happily ever after. I'm *really* into happy endings, Crumsby, aren't you?"

Crumsby mumbled, "Certainly, and as for me, my *belly* has had its own healthy helping of a happy ending."

Well, that just about wraps up my tale. On the thirteenth day of the twelfth month, the Jewish people were saved. They even made a feast to remember everything that had happened—the Feast of Purim. And, yes, Crumsby shows up for it every year!

My dad and I walk through the garden together these days. (It's much more fun walking *with* someone, I found out.) And he was right. It is important what you say and do. Consequences can either harm you or bless you. I'll take the blessing any day. It can make you feel really groovy inside. Kinda like sunshine! Don't *you* think so?

Now that we've imagined how it might be if animals could tell us their tales, go ahead and read God's account of this story in your Bible. You'll find it in Esther 1:1–10:3.

Faith Kids® is an imprint of Cook Communications Ministries,
Colorado Springs, Colorado 80918
Cook Communications, Paris, Ontario
Kingsway Communications, Eastbourne, England

THE PERSIAN PLOT
© 2001 by T. F. Marsh for text and illustrations

Designed by Dana Sherrer of iDesignEtc.
Edited by Kathy Davis

First printing, 2001
Printed in Canada
05 04 03 02 01   5 4 3 2 1

Library of Congress Cataloging-in-Publication Data
Marsh, T. F.

The Persian Plot

Ages: 4-7

My child's need: To grow in courage and learn to stand up for what he or she believes.

Biblical value: Courage

Learning styles: Help your child learn about God's gift of courage in the following ways:

Sight: With your child, look again at the book's illustrations of Queen Esther. Say something like: "Queen Esther was beautiful, wasn't she? But her beauty was on the *outside*. What did she have *inside* that helped her save her people?"
Help your child understand that Esther demonstrated courage. Explain that courage helps us do the right thing, even when we feel afraid or unsure about how things will turn out.

Sound: Read the story aloud to your child. Then talk together about these questions:
• Who helped Esther save the king? (Mordecai)
• Who wanted to kill Mordecai and the Jewish people? (Haman)
• Why was Esther brave to interrupt the king? (It might have made him angry.)
• What reward did the king give Mordecai? (All of the things Haman wanted for himself)
• What special feast today reminds the Jewish people of Esther's courage and God's help? (The Feast of Purim)

Touch: Ask your child to draw a picture of a time when he or she had to be brave like Queen Esther. Talk about ways that God helps us to do the right thing, even when it's hard. Explain that God protected Esther and gave her the wisdom to know what to do. Have your child draw a circle around the picture of himself or herself, to represent how God surrounds us with His care and protection.